The Max Beebnut

Written by
Stephen Rickard

Illustrated by
Richy Sanchez Ayala

Ransom

Chuck was sitting in the coffee bar.
He was waiting for his egg and chips.

It had been a hard week.

The waitress got the food for Chuck.

Picking up his fork, Chuck dug in.
The dish of chips was good!

Then a man sat with Chuck.

The man was looking at Chuck.
He was looking at his dish of chips too.

Looking up, Chuck had a big shock.

The man was Max Beebnut, the big-shot king of You Noob, on the web.

Max Beebnut was the tops.
Yet Max Beebnut was in this coffee
bar, with Chuck! It was nuts!

Then Max took a chip off Chuck's dish of chips and, with a dip in the egg ...

Pop! He bit the chip.

Giving Chuck an odd look, Max got up.

"You can tell that you met me, but they will not admit it was me. Not **the** Max Beebnut, not in **this** coffee bar."

Then Max quit the coffee bar.

Chuck got up to go. He had to tell his pals he had met Max Beebnut.

But Max was right.

Not **the** Max Beebnut,
not in **this** coffee bar.

With a quick look, Chuck sat. Picking up his fork, he dug back in to his egg and chips.